Ninja Foodi XL Pro Grill & Griddle Cookbook for Beginners

Ninja Foodi XL Pro Grill & Griddle Cookbook for Beginners

1000-Day Quick Start & Savory Indoor Grilling,Griddle,Crisp and Bake Recipes for Beginners and Advances Users.

Rhodes Aislin

Table of Contents

INTRODUCTION

The Ninja Foodi smart XL grill is one of the revolutionary cooking appliances that come from the Ninja Family. These 7 in 1 multifunctional cooking appliances not only grill your food but also roast, broil, bake, Air Crisp, and even dehydrate your favourite foods. The body of the appliances is made up of stainless-steel material with an upper domed lid. The accessories like grill grate, BBQ griddle, crisper basket come with ceramic non-stick coating. It works at 1760 watts and produces a maximum of 500°F to 512°F temperature to cook your favorite cooking food.

The Ninja Foodi smart XL grill comes with a large XL cooking pot capacity and is capable of holding 6 pancakes, grilling 6 stakes, 4 sandwiches, and more, which is enough for a large family. You can also use it as a dehydrator and it allows to dehydrate 18 slices at a single cooking cycle. The digital control panel is easy to read and anyone can easily operate the appliances. You just need to select the desired cooking function and set the time and temperature as per your recipe needs. The Ninja Foodi smart XL grill uses rapid hot air circulation techniques to cook food faster and evenly from all sides.

This cookbook contains healthy and delicious Ninja Foodi recipes from breakfast to desserts. The recipes written in this book are simple and written in an easily understandable form. The recipes start with their preparation and cooking time with the step of the instruction set. All the recipes written in this cookbook come with their nutritional values which will help you to keep track of daily calorie consumption. There are very few cookbooks available in the market on this topic thanks for choosing my cookbook. I hope you love and enjoy all the healthy and delicious Ninja Foodi recipes written in this cookbook.

CHAPTER 1: WHAT IS NINJA FOODI SMART GRILL?

The Ninja Foodi smart grill is one of the multifunctional compact-size countertop cooking appliances. It is made with stainless-steel material and works on 1760W power to produce max 500°F heat to cook your food faster. Cooking your food into Ninja Foodi smart grill is one of the healthiest ways of cooking your favorite restaurant meal at home within a few minutes. It air fry your favorite food using up to 75% fewer fats and oil compared with other traditional frying methods. The Ninja Foodi smart grill is loaded with 7 in 1 cooking functions. These functions include a grill, roast, broil, bake, BBQ griddle, Air Crisp and dehydrate. It is one of the versatile cooking appliances specially designed to perform multiple cooking operations. The XL size allows you to cook 6 pancakes, grill 6 stakes, 4 sandwiches, and more which is enough for a large family.

The Ninja Foodi smart grill is equipped with a unique smoke control system that controls grill grate temperature and splatter shield with cool air zone helps to reduce the smoke during the cooking process. The Foodi smart thermometer helps to monitor the internal temperature of the food for perfect doneness. Its closed hood adds an advantage when you cook food on high heat, surround searing, melting, and crisping the cyclonic air cooks your food faster and give you even cooking results. Keep the hood open when you want to sear your food on direct bottom heat.

Features of the Ninja Foodi Smart XL Pro Grill

The Ninja Foodi smart XL pro grill is loaded with various features that other indoor and outdoor grill grates don't have. Using Ninja Foodi Smart XL grill, you can easily serve perfectly cooked food to your friends and family. It allows you to make your food crisp, char-grilled, tender, and juicy. Some of the Ninja Foodi smart pro grill features include:

1. **Foodi XL Pro Powered Grill Grate:** The XL pro powered grill grate comes with a ceramic-coated non-stick grill grate. It is capable of holding 6 stakes at once. Use it with the hood down for high heat cyclonic air for searing and crisping your food faster. Also use it with the hood open for intensely high heat searing. It is ideal for griddle searing, high heat steakhouse grilling, and more. It is the dishwasher-safe grill grate, so it's easy to clean.

2. **Foodi XL Pro Flat top BBQ Griddle:** The flat top BBQ griddle comes with ceramic non-stick coating. Its precise temperature control system cooks your food faster and evenly without hot or cold spots. The flat-top BBQ griddle is not only perfect for breakfast but also used to create savory cheesesteak, hibachi style stir fry, sizzling fajitas, fried rice, smash burgers, and more.

3. **Foodi XL Pro Crisper Basket:** You can use your Ninja Foodi XL pro grill as an air fryer using the crisper basket. The crisper basket comes with ceramic non-stick coating and is ideal for air frying, air crisping, and dehydrating your favorite food. You can make crunchy French fries, onion rings, chicken wings, chicken nuggets, and fried fish.

4. **XL capacity:** The Ninja Foodi smart XL pro grill comes with an extra-large capacity. It is designed to hold 24 hot dogs, 2 pounds of carrot, 6 pancakes, grill 6 stakes, and 4 sandwiches at once without crowding the food. It is enough for a large family.

5. **Smoke Control System:** Most of the indoor grills fill your kitchen with smoke but Ninja Foodi smart XL grill cooks your food without making too much smoke. It comes with precise temperature-controlled grill grates, grease collector, and splatter shield that helps to reduce the smoke. It gives you a smoke-free cooking experience without filling your kitchen with smoke.

6. Smart Thermometer: The Ninja Foodi XL pro grill comes with a smart thermometer that ensures the perfect doneness of food from rare to well. Use a thermometer with 4 smart protein settings and 9 customizable doneness levels. The dual sensor Foodi smart thermometer continuously monitors the food's internal temperature and delivers more accurate cooking results.

7. Easy to clean up: Except for the main unit, most of the other accessories are dishwasher safe. You never need to spend too much time cleaning them. If you don't want to clean them using a dishwasher then you can clean these accessories by using warm, soapy water and use the cleaning brush that comes with appliances.

Functions of Ninja Foodi Smart XL Grill

The Ninja Foodi Smart XL grill is equipped with seven different cooking functions. These functions include a grill, roast, broil, bake, BBQ griddle, the air crisp and dehydrate.

1. Grill: This function is ideal to grill your favorite food, use grill grates to create grill and char marks on your food with grill flavor. Grilling your food is the best way to add flavors and texture to your food. You can use low (400°F), med (450°F), hi (500°F) and max (512°F) settings as per food type. Use low settings for making sausage and bacon, medium settings for sauced meat, marinated foods, and frozen meat, use high settings for chicken, meat, steak, hot dogs, and burgers, use max settings for grilling fruits, vegetables, frozen seafood, and pizzas. Use the open hood to develop char-grilled flavors into your favorite protein. Use a close hood to circulate hot cyclonic air for fast and even cooking results.

2. Roast: Roasting your food is one of the best ways to cook your favorite food with various flavors. The high heat cooks your food with its juices without compromising the taste and texture of the food. This function is ideal for a roasting cut of beef, and pork loin. You can also roast vegetables and fruits like potatoes, eggplants, Brussels sprouts, apples, and pears. Before roasting always coat your veggies with little oil to add more crispiness and even browning results.

3. **Broil:** When broiling your food into Ninja Foodi smart XL grill the direct heat source comes from the top side of the grill. Broiling is one of the fastest cooking methods so you should keep watch on your food when it is cooking. Broiling is ideal for caramelizing your food surface, making it crisp, and then make it deep brown. Using this function you can cook thinner steak, chicken legs, fish fillets, shrimp, scallop, kabobs, bell peppers, zucchini, and pineapples.

4. **Bake:** The Ninja Foodi smart XL grill is capable of baking your favorite cake, cookies, casseroles, fish, cobblers, pastries, pies, and appetizers. While using this function, always check your food not over brown or burn before finishing cooking time. After finishing cooking check your food is done or not by using traditional doneness tests like inserting a toothpick or touching the cake surface to check crumb whether it has been set or not.

5. **BBQ Griddle:** The flat surface ceramic coated BBQ griddle interlock with the grill grate. It unlocks the cooking possibilities beyond breakfast and allows you to create sizzling fajitas, savory cheesesteak, stir-fries, smashes burgers, grilled cheese sandwiches, and more. Open the grill hood for edge-to-edge cooking or close the hood for cyclonic air quick-cooking and crisping toppings. While using this function, use a rubber-tipped spatula to flip your food on the griddle surface, but it may not damage the griddle surface coatings.

6. **Air Crisp:** Air crisper basket exactly fits at the top of the grill grate. When using air crisp function, rapid air circulates the food to make it crispy, crunchy like fried food without adding fats and oil. This function is ideal to make your favorite French fries, chicken nuggets, chicken wings, onion rings, fish sticks, and more. Using this function, you can cook your food by using 75% fats and oils sometimes no oil. The easy-to-use hood allows you to shake or rearrange your food easily.

7. **Dehydrate:** Use this function to remove the moisture from your food to preserve them for a longer time. Use this function to dehydrate your favorite vegetable, fruit, and meat slices. This process works at low temperatures for a longer time. Using this function, you can make your healthy snacks and store them for longer time. To get even dehydrate results make sure food slices are cut into the same size and thickness.

Cleaning and Maintenance

Cleaning is one of the essential processes that keep your appliances clean and hygienic. It also improves the lifecycle of your appliances. The following step-by-step cleaning instruction will help you to clean your Ninja Foodi Smart XL Grill.

1. Before starting the cleaning process unplug the Ninja Foodi grill from the power socket and let it cool down at room temperature. For faster cooling keep the hood of the grill open.

2. Now remove the accessories like grill grate, BBQ griddle, crispier basket, and splatter shield for cleaning. All these accessories are dishwasher safe so you can easily clean them with the dishwasher.

3. You can also hand wash these accessories with the help of a cleaning brush and scrapper that comes with accessories for getting better cleaning results.

4. If still there is any splatter or residue over the grill grate, splatter shield or any other part then soak these accessories into soapy water overnight and then clean them with a cleaning brush.

5. Use a soft damp cloth to clean the main unit from inside and outside.

6. Before placing the accessories at their original position, make sure all these accessories are dry thoroughly.

7. Now your Ninja Foodi smart XL grill is ready for next use.

CHAPTER 2: POULTRY

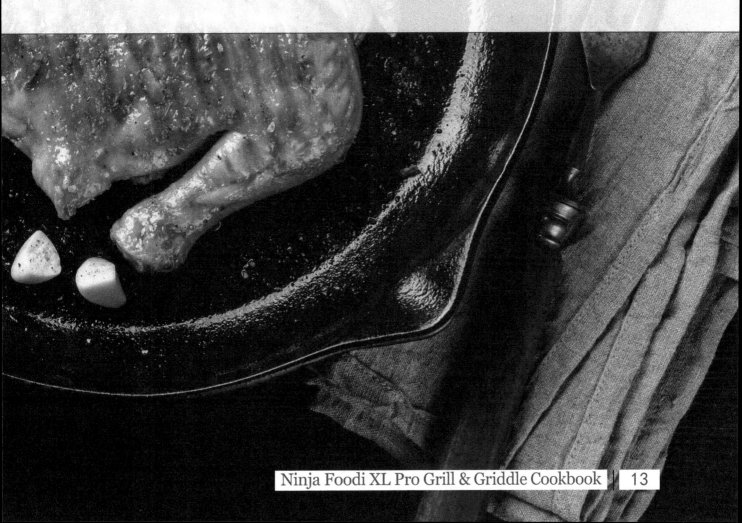

Juicy Chicken Breast

Preparation Time: 10 minutes
Cooking Time: 20 minutes
Serve: 6

Ingredients:

- 1 1/2 lbs chicken breast, boneless
- 1 tsp tomato paste
- 1/2 tsp onion powder
- 1 tsp ground cumin
- 2 lime juice
- 1/4 cup olive oil
- 3 garlic cloves
- 1 tsp paprika
- 2 lime zest
- 2 chipotle peppers
- Salt

Directions:

1. Plug thermometer into the ninja foodi smart XL pro grill unit.
2. Insert grill grate in the unit and close hood.
3. Press GRILL. Set temperature to MED. Press PRESET, then select CHICKEN. Press START/STOP to begin preheating.
4. Add all ingredients except chicken into the blender and blend until well combined.
5. Add chicken into the zip-lock bag and pour blended mixture over chicken. Seal bag and place in refrigerator for overnight.
6. Insert the thermometer into the center of one of the chicken breasts.
7. Once the unit is preheated, place marinated chicken breasts on the grill grate. Close hood.
8. When beeps and display indicate FLIP then flip the chicken. Close hood to continue cooking.

9.Serve and enjoy.

Nutritional Value (Amount per Serving):

- Calories 294
- Fat 19.68 g
- Carbohydrates 5.08 g
- Sugar 1.45 g
- Protein 24.34 g
- Cholesterol 73 mg

Italian Chicken

Preparation Time: 10 minutes
Cooking Time: 10 minutes
Serve: 4

Ingredients:

- 1 lb chicken breasts, boneless & skinless
- 1 tbsp garlic, minced
- 1/2 tsp rosemary
- 1/3 cup olive oil
- 1 tbsp lemon zest
- 1/2 tsp thyme
- 1/3 cup fresh lemon juice
- 1/2 tsp basil
- 2 tsp oregano
- Pepper
- Salt

Directions:

1. Plug thermometer into the ninja foodi smart XL pro grill unit.
2. Insert grill grate in the unit and close hood.
3. Press GRILL. Set temperature to MED. Press PRESET, then select CHICKEN. Press START/STOP to begin to preheat.
4. Add all ingredients except chicken into the zip-lock bag and mix well.
5. Add chicken into the zip-lock bag. Seal bag, shake well, and place in refrigerator for overnight.
6. Insert the thermometer into the center of one of the chicken breasts.
7. Once the unit is preheated, place marinated chicken on the grill grate. Close hood.
8. When beeps and display indicate FLIP then flip the chicken. Close hood to continue cooking.

9.Serve and enjoy.

Nutritional Value (Amount per Serving):

- Calories 367
- Fat 28.44 g
- Carbohydrates 3.68 g
- Sugar 1.22 g
- Protein 24.16 g
- Cholesterol 73 mg

Lemon Pepper Chicken Thighs

Preparation Time: 10 minutes
Cooking Time: 14 minutes
Serve: 2

Ingredients:

- 1 lb chicken thighs, boneless & skinless
- For marinade:
- 1/2 tsp lemon pepper seasoning
- 1/2 tbsp soy sauce
- 1/2 tbsp Dijon mustard
- 1/2 tbsp balsamic vinegar
- 1/2 tsp garlic, minced
- 1/2 tsp dried rosemary
- 1/2 tbsp brown sugar
- 1 1/2 tbsp olive oil

Directions:

1. Plug thermometer into the ninja foodi smart XL pro grill unit.
2. Insert grill grate in the unit and close hood.
3. Press GRILL. Set temperature to MED. Press PRESET, then select CHICKEN. Press START/STOP to begin preheating.
4. Add all marinade ingredients into the zip-lock bag. Add chicken, seal bag and place in refrigerator for overnight.
5. Insert the thermometer into the center of one of the chicken thighs.
6. Once the unit is preheated, place marinated chicken on the grill grate. Close hood.
7. When beeps and display indicate FLIP then flip the chicken. Close hood to continue cooking.
8. Serve and enjoy.

Nutritional Value (Amount per Serving):

- Calories 625
- Fat 48.74 g
- Carbohydrates 4.92 g
- Sugar 2.4 g
- Protein 39.45 g
- Cholesterol 226 mg

Marinated Chicken

Preparation Time: 10 minutes
Cooking Time: 12 minutes
Serve: 6

Ingredients:

- 1 ½ lbs chicken breasts
- 2 tbsp fresh lemon juice
- 1/4 cup Worcestershire sauce
- 1/4 cup soy sauce
- 1/2 cup balsamic vinegar
- 1/2 cup olive oil
- 2 tsp garlic powder
- 1/2 tsp black pepper
- 2 tbsp Dijon mustard
- 2 tsp dried rosemary
- 3/4 cup brown sugar
- 2 tsp salt

Directions:

1. Plug thermometer into the ninja foodi smart XL pro grill unit.
2. Insert grill grate in the unit and close hood.
3. Press GRILL. Set temperature to MED. Press PRESET, then select CHICKEN. Press START/STOP to begin to preheat.
4. Add chicken and remaining ingredients into the zip-lock bag. Seal bag, shake well, and place in refrigerator for overnight.
5. Insert the thermometer into the center of one of the chicken breasts.
6. Once the unit is preheated, place marinated chicken on the grill grate. Close hood.
7. When beeps and display indicate FLIP then flip the chicken. Close hood to continue cooking.
8. Serve and enjoy.

Nutritional Value (Amount per Serving):

- Calories 526
- Fat 30.63 g
- Carbohydrates 37.08 g
- Sugar 33.26 g
- Protein 24.95 g
- Cholesterol 73 mg

Flavors Orange Chicken

Preparation Time: 10 minutes
Cooking Time: 10 minutes
Serve: 4

Ingredients:

- 1 lb chicken breasts, boneless & skinless
- 1/2 cup orange juice
- 1 garlic clove, minced
- 3 tbsp olive oil
- 1/2 tsp allspice
- 3/4 tsp ground nutmeg

Directions:

1. Plug thermometer into the ninja foodi smart XL pro grill unit.
2. Insert grill grate in the unit and close hood.
3. Press GRILL. Set temperature to MED. Press PRESET, then select CHICKEN. Press START/STOP to begin to preheat.
4. Add chicken and remaining ingredients into the zip-lock bag. Seal bag and place in refrigerator for 4 hours.
5. Insert the thermometer into the center of one of the chicken breasts.
6. Once the unit is preheated, place marinated chicken on the grill grate. Close hood.
7. When beeps and display indicate FLIP then flip the chicken. Close hood to continue cooking.
8. Serve and enjoy.

Nutritional Value (Amount per Serving):

- Calories 304
- Fat 20.83 g
- Carbohydrates 4.23 g
- Sugar 2.61 g
- Protein 23.94 g
- Cholesterol 73 mg

Curried Chicken Breasts

Preparation Time: 10 minutes
Cooking Time: 10 minutes
Serve: 4

Ingredients:

- 1 lb chicken breasts, boneless & skinless
- 1 1/2 tbsp Thai red curry
- 1 tsp brown sugar
- 1 1/2 tbsp fish sauce
- 1/2 cup coconut milk

Directions:

1. Plug thermometer into the ninja foodi smart XL pro grill unit.
2. Insert grill grate in the unit and close hood.
3. Press GRILL. Set temperature to MED. Press PRESET, then select CHICKEN. Press START/STOP to begin to preheat.
4. Add chicken and remaining ingredients into the zip-lock bag. Seal bag and place in refrigerator for 8 hours.
5. Insert the thermometer into the center of one of the chicken breasts.
6. Once the unit is preheated, place marinated chicken on the grill grate. Close hood.
7. When beeps and display indicate FLIP then flip the chicken. Close hood to continue cooking.
8. Serve and enjoy.

Nutritional Value (Amount per Serving):

- Calories 278
- Fat 17.97 g
- Carbohydrates 4.36 g
- Sugar 2.43 g
- Protein 25.01 g
- Cholesterol 73 mg

Easy Pesto Chicken

Preparation Time: 10 minutes
Cooking Time: 10 minutes
Serve: 4

Ingredients:

- 1 lb chicken breasts, boneless & skinless
- 1 tbsp olive oil
- 3/4 cup pesto
- Pepper
- Salt

Directions:

1. Plug thermometer into the ninja foodi smart XL pro grill unit.
2. Insert grill grate in the unit and close hood.
3. Press GRILL. Set temperature to MED. Press PRESET, then select CHICKEN. Press START/STOP to begin preheating.
4. Add chicken and remaining ingredients into the zip-lock bag. Seal bag and place into refrigerator for 4 hours.
5. Insert the thermometer into the center of one of the chicken breasts.
6. Once the unit is preheated, place marinated chicken on the grill grate. Close hood.
7. When beeps and display indicate FLIP then flip the chicken. Close hood to continue cooking.
8. Serve and enjoy.

Nutritional Value (Amount per Serving):

- Calories 478
- Fat 39.4 g
- Carbohydrates 2.92 g
- Sugar 0.95 g
- Protein 28.41 g
- Cholesterol 80 mg

Grill Chicken Patties

Preparation Time: 10 minutes
Cooking Time: 10 minutes
Serve: 4

Ingredients:

- 1 egg, lightly beaten
- 1 lb ground chicken
- 1 jalapeno, chopped
- 1/2 cup bacon, cooked & chopped
- 1/2 cup mozzarella cheese, shredded
- Pepper
- Salt

Directions:

1. Plug thermometer into the ninja foodi smart XL pro grill unit.
2. Insert grill grate in the unit and close hood.
3. Press GRILL. Set temperature to MED. Press PRESET, then select CHICKEN. Press START/STOP to begin preheating.
4. Add chicken and remaining ingredients into the mixing bowl and mix until well combined.
5. Make patties from the chicken mixture.
6. Insert the thermometer into the center of one of the chicken patties.
7. Once the unit is preheated, place chicken patties on the grill grate. Close hood.
8. When beeps and display indicate FLIP then flip chicken patties. Close hood to continue cooking.
9. Serve and enjoy.

Nutritional Value (Amount per Serving):

- Calories 277
- Fat 16.96 g
- Carbohydrates 3.46 g
- Sugar 1.24 g
- Protein 28.71 g
- Cholesterol 255 mg

Sweet Chicken Tenderloins

Preparation Time: 10 minutes
Cooking Time: 10 minutes
Serve: 3

Ingredients:

- 1 1/2 lbs chicken tenderloins
- 2 tbsp honey
- 3 tbsp ketchup
- 1/4 cup soy sauce
- 2 tbsp olive oil
- 4 garlic cloves, minced
- 2 tbsp brown sugar
- 1/4 cup pineapple juice

Directions:

1. Plug thermometer into the ninja foodi smart XL pro grill unit.
2. Insert grill grate in the unit and close hood.
3. Press GRILL. Set temperature to MED. Press PRESET, then select CHICKEN. Press START/STOP to begin preheating.
4. Add chicken and remaining ingredients into the zip-lock bag. Seal bag and place in the refrigerator overnight.
5. Insert the thermometer into the center of one of the chicken tenderloins.
6. Once the unit is preheated, place marinated chicken on the grill grate. Close hood.
7. When beeps and display indicate FLIP then flip the chicken. Close hood to continue cooking.
8. Serve and enjoy.

Nutritional Value (Amount per Serving):

- Calories 479
- Fat 19.02 g
- Carbohydrates 28.15 g
- Sugar 24.32 g
- Protein 48.19 g
- Cholesterol 147 mg

Mexican Chicken

Preparation Time: 10 minutes
Cooking Time: 16 minutes
Serve: 4

Ingredients:

- 1 lb chicken breasts, boneless & skinless
- 1/2 tsp cumin
- 1/4 cup olive oil
- 1 tsp chili powder
- 1/4 cup cilantro, chopped
- 2 garlic cloves, minced
- 1 lime juice
- 1/4 tsp pepper
- 1/2 tsp salt

Directions:

1. Plug thermometer into the ninja foodi smart XL pro grill unit.
2. Insert grill grate in the unit and close hood.
3. Press GRILL. Set temperature to MED. Press PRESET then select CHICKEN. Press START/STOP to begin preheating.
4. Add chicken and remaining ingredients into the zip-lock bag. Seal bag and place in refrigerator for 4 hours.
5. Insert the thermometer into the center of one of the chicken breasts.
6. Once the unit is preheated, place marinated chicken on the grill grate. Close hood.
7. When beeps and display indicate FLIP then flip the chicken. Close hood to continue cooking.
8. Serve and enjoy.

Nutritional Value (Amount per Serving):

- Calories 324
- Fat 24.17 g
- Carbohydrates 2.18 g
- Sugar 0.41 g
- Protein 24 g
- Cholesterol 73 mg

Crispy Chicken Wings

Preparation Time: 10 minutes
Cooking Time: 30 minutes
Serve: 8

Ingredients:

- 2 lbs chicken wings
- 1 tsp paprika
- 1 tbsp chili powder
- 1/4 cup butter, melted
- 1 tsp garlic powder
- 1 tsp black pepper
- 1 tbsp brown sugar
- 1 tsp salt

Directions:

1. Place crisper basket on the grill grate and close hood.
2. Press AIR CRISP button. Set temperature to 400 F and set the time for 30 minutes. Press START/STOP to begin preheating.
3. In a large bowl, toss chicken wings with remaining ingredients until well coated.
4. Once the unit is preheated, then add chicken wings in crisper basket. Close hood to start cooking.
5. Turn chicken wings halfway through.
6. Serve and enjoy.

Nutritional Value (Amount per Serving):

- Calories 201
- Fat 9.97 g
- Carbohydrates 1.56 g
- Sugar 0.51 g
- Protein 25.25 g
- Cholesterol 80 mg

Meatballs

Preparation Time: 10 minutes
Cooking Time: 10 minutes
Serve: 4

Ingredients:

- 1 egg, lightly beaten
- 1 1/2 lbs ground turkey
- 1 bell pepper, chopped
- 1 tbsp fresh coriander, minced
- 1/4 cup fresh parsley, minced
- ½ tsp chili powder
- Pepper
- Salt

Directions:

1. Place crisper basket on the grill grate and close hood.
2. Press AIR CRISP button. Set temperature to 400 F and set the time for 10 minutes. Press START/STOP to begin preheating.
3. In a bowl, mix together ground turkey and remaining ingredients until well combined.
4. Make small balls from the turkey mixture.
5. Once the unit is preheated, then add meatballs in crisper basket. Close hood to start cooking.
6. Turn meatballs halfway through.
7. Serve and enjoy.

Nutritional Value (Amount per Serving):

- Calories 296
- Fat 15.57 g
- Carbohydrates 2.8 g
- Sugar 1.37 g
- Protein 36.3 g
- Cholesterol 272 mg

Flavors Chicken Drumsticks

Preparation Time: 10 minutes
Cooking Time: 25 minutes
Serve: 6

Ingredients:

- 1 1/2 lbs chicken drumsticks
- 1 tsp olive oil
- 1/4 tsp ground cumin
- 1/2 tsp dried oregano
- 1/4 tsp onion powder
- 1 tsp honey mustard sauce
- 1/2 tsp garlic powder
- 1 tbsp butter, melted
- 1/4 tsp cayenne
- 1 tsp paprika
- 1 tsp dried parsley
- Pepper
- Salt

Directions:

1. Place crisper basket on the grill grate and close hood.
2. Press AIR CRISP button. Set temperature to 375 F and time for 25 minutes. Press START/STOP to begin preheating.
3. In a bowl, toss chicken drumsticks with remaining ingredients until well coated.
4. Once the unit is preheated, then add chicken drumsticks in crisper basket. Close hood to start cooking.
5. Serve and enjoy.

Nutritional Value (Amount per Serving):

- Calories 216
- Fat 13.55 g
- Carbohydrates 1.67 g
- Sugar 0.58 g
- Protein 20.83 g
- Cholesterol 110 mg

Turkey Burger Patties

Preparation Time: 10 minutes
Cooking Time: 15 minutes
Serve: 5

Ingredients:

- 1 lb ground turkey
- 1 tsp onion powder
- 8 mushrooms, finely chopped
- 1 tsp garlic powder
- 1 tbsp Worcestershire sauce
- 1/4 cup cilantro, chopped
- Pepper
- Salt

Directions:

1. Place crisper basket on the grill grate and close hood.
2. Press AIR CRISP button. Set temperature to 380 F and time for 15 minutes. Press START/STOP to begin preheating.
3. Add ground turkey and remaining ingredients into the mixing bowl and mix until well combined.
4. Make patties from the meat mixture.
5. Once the unit is preheated, then place patties in crisper basket. Close hood to start cooking.
6. Turn patties halfway through.
7. Serve and enjoy.

Nutritional Value (Amount per Serving):

- Calories 151
- Fat 7.08 g
- Carbohydrates 3.31 g
- Sugar 1.42 g
- Protein 19.08 g
- Cholesterol 63 mg

Juicy Turkey Breast

Preparation Time: 10 minutes
Cooking Time: 45 minutes
Serve: 4

Ingredients:

- 2 lbs turkey breast
- 1 tbsp peppercorn, grinded
- 1/4 cup butter, melted
- 2 tbsp thyme, chopped
- 2 tbsp garlic, minced
- 1 tbsp sea salt

Directions:

1. Place crisper basket on the grill grate and close hood.
2. Press AIR CRISP button. Set temperature to 375 F and time for 45 minutes. Press START/STOP to begin preheating.
3. In a small bowl, mix butter, thyme, peppercorn, garlic, and salt.
4. Brush turkey breast with butter mixture
5. Once the unit is preheated, then place turkey breast in crisper basket. Close hood to start cooking.
6. Slice and serve.

Nutritional Value (Amount per Serving):

- Calories 484
- Fat 29.54 g
- Carbohydrates 1.82 g
- Sugar 0.13 g
- Protein 50.14 g
- Cholesterol 180 mg

Miso Chicken Thighs

Preparation Time: 10 minutes
Cooking Time: 20 minutes
Serve: 4

Ingredients:

- 4 chicken thighs, boneless
- 1 tbsp soy sauce
- 1 tbsp rice wine
- 1 tbsp mirin
- 3 tbsp miso

Directions:

1. Place crisper basket on the grill grate and close hood.
2. Press AIR CRISP button. Set temperature to 380 F and time for 20 minutes. Press START/STOP to begin preheating.
3. In a mixing bowl, mix chicken with rice wine, soy sauce, mirin, and miso until well coated. Cover and place in refrigerator for overnight.
4. Once the unit is preheated, then place chicken in crisper basket. Close hood to start cooking.
5. Serve and enjoy.

Nutritional Value (Amount per Serving):

- Calories 469
- Fat 33.93 g
- Carbohydrates 5.77 g
- Sugar 1.58 g
- Protein 33.91 g
- Cholesterol 189 mg

Chicken Meatballs

Preparation Time: 10 minutes
Cooking Time: 16 minutes
Serve: 4

Ingredients:

- 1 egg
- 1 lb ground chicken
- 1 tsp garlic powder
- 1 oz parmesan cheese, shredded
- 1/4 cup breadcrumbs
- 2 tbsp sweet chili sauce
- 1 tsp chili powder
- 1 tsp ground ginger
- Pepper
- Salt

Directions:

1. Place crisper basket on the grill grate and close hood.
2. Press AIR CRISP button. Set temperature to 400 F and time for 16 minutes. Press START/STOP to begin preheating.
3. In a mixing bowl, mix chicken with remaining ingredients until well combined.
4. Make small balls from chicken mixture.
5. Once the unit is preheated, then place meatballs in crisper basket. Close hood to start cooking.
6. Turn meatballs halfway through.
7. Serve and enjoy.

Nutritional Value (Amount per Serving):

- Calories 244
- Fat 13.74 g
- Carbohydrates 5.26 g
- Sugar 1.72 g
- Protein 24.73 g
- Cholesterol 258 mg

Balsamic Chicken Thighs

Preparation Time: 10 minutes
Cooking Time: 14 minutes
Serve: 4

Ingredients:

- 4 chicken thighs, boneless
- 1 tsp dried rosemary
- 1/4 cup fresh lemon juice
- 1/4 cup balsamic vinaigrette
- 1/4 cup Dijon mustard
- Pepper
- Salt

Directions:

1. Place crisper basket on the grill grate and close hood.
2. Press AIR CRISP button. Set temperature to 400 F and time for 14 minutes. Press START/STOP to begin preheating.
3. Add chicken and remaining ingredients into the zip-lock bag. Seal bag and place in refrigerator for 2 hours.
4. Once the unit is preheated, then place marinated chicken in crisper basket. Close hood to start cooking.
5. Serve and enjoy.

Nutritional Value (Amount per Serving):

- Calories 445
- Fat 32.66g
- Carbohydrates 3.83 g
- Sugar 1.1 g
- Protein 32.83 g
- Cholesterol 189 mg

Easy Chicken Legs

Preparation Time: 10 minutes
Cooking Time: 18 minutes
Serve: 6

Ingredients:

- 2 lbs chicken drumsticks
- 2 tbsp olive oil
- 1 tbsp baking powder
- 1 cup pickle brine
- 2 tsp smoked paprika
- 1/2 tsp dried rosemary
- 1 tsp garlic powder
- Pepper
- Salt

Directions:

1. Place crisper basket on the grill grate and close hood.
2. Press AIR CRISP button. Set temperature to 400 F and time for 18 minutes. Press START/STOP to begin preheating.
3. In a mixing bowl, add chicken drumsticks and pickle brine. Cover and place in refrigerator for 2 hours.
4. In a shallow dish, mix together baking powder, rosemary, paprika, garlic powder, pepper, and salt.
5. Remove chicken drumsticks from marinade and brush with oil and coat with baking powder mixture.
6. Once the unit is preheated, then place chicken drumsticks in crisper basket. Close hood to start cooking.
7. Serve and enjoy.

Nutritional Value (Amount per Serving):

- Calories 295
- Fat 18.61 g
- Carbohydrates 3.43 g
- Sugar 0.73 g
- Protein 27.8 g
- Cholesterol 139 mg

Spicy Chipotle Chicken Breast

Preparation Time: 10 minutes
Cooking Time: 18 minutes
Serve: 2

Ingredients:

- 2 chicken breasts, boneless
- 2 tbsp olive oil
- 1 tbsp brown sugar
- 2 tsp chipotle chili pepper powder
- 3 tbsp can adobo sauce
- 1/2 tsp dried oregano
- 1 tsp onion powder
- 1 tsp garlic powder
- Salt

Directions:

1. Place crisper basket on the grill grate and close hood.
2. Press AIR CRISP button. Set temperature to 360 F and time for 18 minutes. Press START/STOP to begin preheating.
3. Add chicken and remaining ingredients into the zip-lock bag. Seal bag and place in refrigerator for 4 hours.
4. Once the unit is preheated, then place marinated chicken in crisper basket. Close hood to start cooking.
5. Serve and enjoy.

Nutritional Value (Amount per Serving):

- Calories 643
- Fat 40.41 g
- Carbohydrates 5.89 g
- Sugar 2.87 g
- Protein 61.32 g
- Cholesterol 186 mg

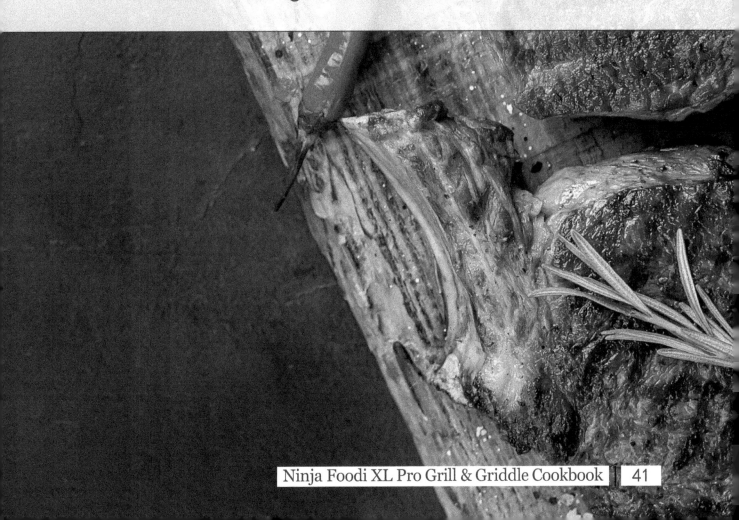

CHAPTER 3: MEAT RECIPES

Flavorful Steak

Preparation Time: 10 minutes
Cooking Time: 10 minutes
Serve: 4

Ingredients:

- 1 1/2 lbs skirt steak
- 3 garlic cloves, chopped
- 1 onion, chopped
- 1/3 cup lime juice
- 1 cup cilantro, chopped
- 1/2 tsp pepper
- 1/2 cup pickled jalapenos, sliced
- 2 tbsp olive oil
- 1/2 tsp salt

Directions:

1. Plug thermometer into the ninja foodi smart XL pro grill unit.
2. Insert grill grate in the unit and close hood.
3. Press GRILL. Set temperature to MED. Press PRESET, then select BEEF. Press START/STOP to begin preheating.
4. Add cilantro, oil, jalapenos, lime juice, garlic, pepper, and salt to the blender and blend until smooth.
5. Add steak into the large bowl. Pour blended mixture over steak and coat well. Cover and place in refrigerator for 2 hours
6. Insert the thermometer into the center of one of the steaks.
7. Once the unit is preheated, place steak on the grill grate. Close hood.
8. When beeps and display indicate FLIP then flip the steak. Close hood to continue cooking.
9. Serve and enjoy.

Nutritional Value (Amount per Serving):

- Calories 460
- Fat 27.37 g
- Carbohydrates 6.4 g
- Sugar 2.31 g
- Protein 45.28 g
- Cholesterol 102 mg

Tasty Lamb Chops

Preparation Time: 10 minutes
Cooking Time: 10 minutes
Serve: 6

Ingredients:

- 12 lamb chops
- 1 tbsp brown sugar
- 1 tbsp turmeric
- 1/2 tsp ground coriander
- 1 tbsp chili powder
- 1 tsp kosher salt

Directions:

1. Plug thermometer into the ninja foodi smart XL pro grill unit.
2. Insert grill grate in the unit and close hood.
3. Press GRILL. Set temperature to MED. Press PRESET, then select LAMB. Press START/STOP to begin preheating.
4. In a small bowl, mix together sugar, turmeric, coriander, chili powder, and salt and rub all over lamb chops
5. Insert the thermometer into the center of one of the lamb chops.
6. Once the unit is preheated, place lamb chops on the grill grate. Close hood.
7. When beeps and display indicate FLIP then flip lamb chops. Close hood to continue cooking.
8. Serve and enjoy.

Nutritional Value (Amount per Serving):

- Calories 1299
- Fat 62.66 g
- Carbohydrates 2.24 g
- Sugar 0.66 g
- Protein 181.59 g
- Cholesterol 599 mg

Creole Herb Lamb Chops

Preparation Time: 10 minutes
Cooking Time: 10 minutes
Serve: 6

Ingredients:

- 6 lamb chops
- 1 tsp Creole seasoning
- 1/2 tsp garlic, minced
- 1 tsp ground white pepper
- 1 tsp thyme, minced
- 1 tbsp fresh rosemary, minced
- Pepper
- Salt

Directions:

1. Plug thermometer into the ninja foodi smart XL pro grill unit.
2. Insert grill grate in the unit and close hood.
3. Press GRILL. Set temperature to MED. Press PRESET, then select LAMB. Press START/STOP to begin preheating.
4. Season lamb chops with pepper and salt and set aside.
5. In a small bowl, mix together white pepper, Creole seasoning, thyme, garlic, and rosemary and rub over lamb chops.
6. Insert the thermometer into the center of one of the lamb chops.
7. Once the unit is preheated, place lamb chops on the grill grate. Close hood.
8. When beeps and display indicate FLIP then flip lamb chops. Close hood to continue cooking.
9. Serve and enjoy.

Nutritional Value (Amount per Serving):

- Calories 653
- Fat 31.26 g
- Carbohydrates 1.87 g
- Sugar 0.82 g
- Protein 90.98 g
- Cholesterol 299 mg

Lemon Pork Chops

Preparation Time: 10 minutes
Cooking Time: 10 minutes
Serve: 2

Ingredients:

- 2 pork chops
- For marinade:
- 1 tbsp brown sugar
- 1/3 cup olive oil
- 1/2 tsp oregano
- 1/4 cup soy sauce
- 1/4 cup lemon juice
- 1 tsp onion powder
- Pepper

Directions:

1. Plug thermometer into the ninja foodi smart XL pro grill unit.
2. Insert grill grate in the unit and close hood.
3. Press GRILL. Set temperature to MED. Press PRESET, then select PORK. Press START/STOP to begin preheating.
4. Add marinade and pork chops into the zip-lock bag. Seal bag and place in the refrigerator for overnight.
5. Insert the thermometer into the center of one of the pork chops.
6. Once the unit is preheated, place marinated pork chops on the grill grate. Close hood.
7. When beeps and display indicate FLIP then flip pork chops. Close hood to continue cooking.
8. Serve and enjoy.

Nutritional Value (Amount per Serving):

- Calories 771
- Fat 58.92 g
- Carbohydrates 16.94 g
- Sugar 10.69 g
- Protein 43.19 g
- Cholesterol 132 mg

Easy Pork Chops

Preparation Time: 10 minutes
Cooking Time: 10 minutes
Serve: 4

Ingredients:

- 4 pork chops, boneless
- 1 tbsp olive oil
- For seasoning:
- 1/4 tsp dried basil
- 1/4 tsp garlic powder
- 1/4 tsp dried onion, minced
- 1/4 tsp dried parsley
- Salt

Directions:

1. Plug thermometer into the ninja foodi smart XL pro grill unit.
2. Insert grill grate in the unit and close hood.
3. Press GRILL. Set temperature to MED. Press PRESET, then select PORK. Press START/STOP to begin preheating.
4. In a small bowl, mix together all seasoning ingredients.
5. Brush pork chops with oil and rub with seasoning.
6. Insert the thermometer into the center of one of the pork chops.
7. Once the unit is preheated, place pork chops on the grill grate. Close hood.
8. When beeps and display indicate FLIP then flip pork chops. Close hood to continue cooking.
9. Serve and enjoy.

Nutritional Value (Amount per Serving):

- Calories 368
- Fat 20.76 g
- Carbohydrates 2.16 g
- Sugar 1.12 g
- Protein 40.45 g
- Cholesterol 132 mg

Lamb Burger Patties

Preparation Time: 10 minutes
Cooking Time: 8 minutes
Serve: 4

Ingredients:

- 1 lb ground lamb
- 10 fresh mint leaves
- 1/4 cup fresh parsley
- 1 tsp dried oregano
- 1 cup feta cheese, crumbled
- 3 garlic cloves
- 1 jalapeno pepper, remove seeds
- 8 fresh basil leaves
- Pepper
- Salt

Directions:

1. Plug thermometer into the ninja foodi smart XL pro grill unit.
2. Insert grill grate in the unit and close hood.
3. Press GRILL. Set temperature to MED. Press PRESET, then select LAMB. Press START/STOP to begin preheating.
4. Add garlic, mint, jalapeno, basil, and parsley into the blender and blend until smooth.
5. Add ground lamb, crumbled cheese, oregano, blended garlic mixture, pepper, and salt into the bowl and mix until well combined.
6. Make patties from lamb mixture.
7. Insert the thermometer into the center of one of the lamb patties.
8. Once the unit is preheated, place lamb patties on the grill grate. Close hood.
9. When beeps and display indicate FLIP then flip patties. Close hood to continue cooking.
10. Serve and enjoy.

Nutritional Value (Amount per Serving):

- Calories 331
- Fat 22.18 g
- Carbohydrates 4.21 g
- Sugar 2.32 g
- Protein 29.18 g
- Cholesterol 105 mg

Spicy Lemon Lamb Chops

Preparation Time: 10 minutes
Cooking Time: 12 minutes
Serve: 4

Ingredients:

- 8 lamb chops
- 1 tbsp garlic, minced
- 2 tbsp lemon juice
- 2 tbsp Harris
- 3/4 tsp ground cumin
- Pepper
- Salt

Directions:

1. Plug thermometer into the ninja foodi smart XL pro grill unit.
2. Insert grill grate in the unit and close hood.
3. Press GRILL. Set temperature to MED. Press PRESET, then select PORK. Press START/STOP to begin preheating.
4. Add lamb chops and remaining ingredients into the zip-lock bag. Seal bag and place in the refrigerator for 2 hours.
5. Insert the thermometer into the center of one of the lamb chops.
6. Once the unit is preheated, place lamb chops on the grill grate. Close hood.
7. When beeps and display indicate FLIP then flip lamb chops. Close hood to continue cooking.
8. Serve and enjoy.

Nutritional Value (Amount per Serving):

- Calories 1299
- Fat 62.56 g
- Carbohydrates 2.47 g
- Sugar 0.8 g
- Protein 181.72 g
- Cholesterol 599 mg

Marinated Pork Chops

Preparation Time: 10 minutes
Cooking Time: 12 minutes
Serve: 4

Ingredients:

- 4 pork chops
- 2 tbsp grainy mustard
- 2 tbsp Dijon mustard
- 1/4 cup honey
- 3 garlic cloves, chopped
- 1 tbsp soy sauce
- 2 tbsp vinegar
- Pepper
- Salt

Directions:

1. Plug thermometer into the ninja foodi smart XL pro grill unit.
2. Insert grill grate in the unit and close hood.
3. Press GRILL. Set temperature to MED. Press PRESET, then select PORK. Press START/STOP to begin preheating.
4. Add pork chops and remaining ingredients into the zip-lock bag. Seal bag and place in the refrigerator for 2 hours.
5. Insert the thermometer into the center of one of the pork chops.
6. Once the unit is preheated, place marinated pork chops on the grill grate. Close hood.
7. When beeps and display indicate FLIP then flip pork chops. Close hood to continue cooking.
8. Serve and enjoy.

Nutritional Value (Amount per Serving):

- Calories 423
- Fat 18.64 g
- Carbohydrates 21.24 g
- Sugar 18.95 g
- Protein 41.5 g
- Cholesterol 132 mg

Easy BBQ Pork Chops

Preparation Time: 10 minutes
Cooking Time: 14 minutes
Serve: 4

Ingredients:

- 4 pork loin chops
- 2 tbsp brown sugar
- 1 tsp pepper
- 1/2 tsp cayenne
- ¼ tsp chili powder
- 1/2 tsp ground mustard
- 1 tsp paprika
- 2 tsp kosher salt

Directions:

1. Plug thermometer into the ninja foodi smart XL pro grill unit.
2. Insert grill grate in the unit and close hood.
3. Press GRILL. Set temperature to MED. Press PRESET, then select PORK. Press START/STOP to begin preheating.
4. In a small bowl, mix together sugar, pepper, cayenne, mustard, paprika, chili powder, and salt and rub over pork chops.
5. Insert the thermometer into the center of one of the pork chops.
6. Once the unit is preheated, place pork chops on the grill grate. Close hood.
7. When beeps and display indicate FLIP then flip pork chops. Close hood to continue cooking.
8. Serve and enjoy.

Nutritional Value (Amount per Serving):

- Calories 343
- Fat 17.62 g
- Carbohydrates 3.23 g
- Sugar 2.24 g
- Protein 40.63 g
- Cholesterol 132 mg

Pork Shoulder Steak

Preparation Time: 10 minutes
Cooking Time: 10 minutes
Serve: 4

Ingredients:

- 4 pork shoulder steaks
- 2 tbsp parsley
- 1 onion, sliced
- 1 tbsp vinegar
- 1/3 cup olive oil
- 1 1/2 tsp oregano
- 1 tsp paprika
- 1 tsp ground cumin
- 1/2 tsp fresh thyme
- Pepper
- Salt

Directions:

1. Plug thermometer into the ninja foodi smart XL pro grill unit.
2. Insert grill grate in the unit and close hood.
3. Press GRILL. Set temperature to MED. Press PRESET, then select PORK. Press START/STOP to begin preheating.
4. Add pork steaks and remaining ingredients into the zip-lock bag. Seal bag and place in the refrigerator overnight.
5. Insert the thermometer into the center of one of the steaks.
6. Once the unit is preheated, place steaks on the grill grate. Close hood.
7. When beeps and display indicate FLIP then flip steaks. Close hood to continue cooking.
8. Serve and enjoy.

Nutritional Value (Amount per Serving):

- Calories 663
- Fat 50.8 g
- Carbohydrates 2.25 g
- Sugar 0.79 g
- Protein 46.9 g
- Cholesterol 181 mg

Horseradish Pork Chops

Preparation Time: 10 minutes
Cooking Time: 20 minutes
Serve: 4

Ingredients:

- 4 pork chops, boneless
- 2 tsp olive oil
- 1/4 tsp black pepper
- 1 tbsp ground coriander
- 1 1/2 tbsp prepared horseradish
- 1/2 tsp salt

Directions:

1. Place crisper basket on the grill grate and close hood.
2. Press AIR CRISP button. Set temperature to 350 F and time for 20 minutes. Press START/STOP to begin preheating.
3. In a small bowl, mix together coriander, oil, horseradish, pepper, and salt and rub all over pork chops.
4. Once the unit is preheated, then place pork chops in crisper basket. Close hood to start cooking.
5. Flip Pork chops halfway through.
6. Serve and enjoy.

Nutritional Value (Amount per Serving):

- Calories 351
- Fat 19.66 g
- Carbohydrates 0.76 g
- Sugar 0.45 g
- Protein 40.3 g
- Cholesterol 132 mg

Lamb Patties

Preparation Time: 10 minutes
Cooking Time: 12 minutes
Serve: 8

Ingredients:

- 2 lbs ground lamb
- 1/2 tsp cinnamon
- 2 tbsp fresh parsley, chopped
- 1 tsp garlic, minced
- 1 tsp paprika
- 1 tbsp ground cumin
- 1 tbsp ground coriander
- Pepper
- Salt

Directions:

1. Place crisper basket on the grill grate and close hood.
2. Press AIR CRISP button. Set temperature to 400 F and time for 12 minutes. Press START/STOP to begin preheating.
3. Add ground meat and remaining ingredients into the mixing bowl and mix until well combined.
4. Make patties from the meat mixture.
5. Once the unit is preheated, then place patties in crisper basket. Close hood to start cooking.
6. Turn patties halfway through.
7. Serve and enjoy.

Nutritional Value (Amount per Serving):

- Calories 226
- Fat 14.3 g
- Carbohydrates 1.33 g
- Sugar 0.35 g
- Protein 23.4 g
- Cholesterol 71 mg

Meatballs

Preparation Time: 10 minutes
Cooking Time: 15 minutes
Serve: 4

Ingredients:

- 1 lb ground beef
- 1 tsp Italian seasoning
- 2 tsp Worcestershire sauce
- 1 tbsp parsley, chopped
- 2 tbsp onion, chopped
- 2 garlic cloves, minced
- 1 tsp salt

Directions:

1. Place crisper basket on the grill grate and close hood.
2. Press AIR CRISP button. Set temperature to 350 F and time for 15 minutes. Press START/STOP to begin preheating.
3. In a bowl, mix together meat and remaining ingredients until well combined.
4. Make small balls from meat mixture.
5. Once the unit is preheated then place meatballs in crisper basket. Close hood to start cooking.
6. Serve and enjoy.

Nutritional Value (Amount per Serving):

- Calories 297
- Fat 18.36 g
- Carbohydrates 2 g
- Sugar 0.6 g
- Protein 28.84 g
- Cholesterol 100 mg

Asian Pork Chops

Preparation Time: 10 minutes
Cooking Time: 12 minutes
Serve: 2

Ingredients:

- 2 pork chops, boneless
- 1/2 tsp cinnamon
- 1 tbsp water
- 1 tbsp rice wine
- 1 tbsp dark soy sauce
- 1/2 tsp five-spice powder
- 1 tsp black pepper
- 1 1/2 tbsp sugar
- 1 tbsp light soy sauce

Directions:

1. Place crisper basket on the grill grate and close hood.
2. Press AIR CRISP button. Set temperature to 380 F and time for 12 minutes. Press START/STOP to begin preheating.
3. Add pork chops and remaining ingredients into the zip-lock bag. Seal bag and place in refrigerator for 2 hours.
4. Once the unit is preheated, then place marinated pork chops in crisper basket. Close hood to start cooking.
5. Serve and enjoy.

Nutritional Value (Amount per Serving):

- Calories 379
- Fat 18.24 g
- Carbohydrates 10.54 g
- Sugar 6.04 g
- Protein 42.23g
- Cholesterol 132 mg

Flavorful Steak

Preparation Time: 10 minutes
Cooking Time: 10 minutes
Serve: 4

Ingredients:

- 1 lb flank steak, sliced
- 1/3 cup cilantro, chopped
- 1 tsp olive oil
- 4 tsp soy sauce
- 1/4 tsp cayenne
- 3 tbsp lime juice
- 2 tsp chili powder
- 1 tsp cumin
- 1/4 tsp salt

Directions:

1. Place crisper basket on the grill grate and close hood.
2. Press AIR CRISP button. Set temperature to 380 F and time for 10 minutes. Press START/STOP to begin preheating.
3. Add steak pieces and remaining ingredients into the zip-lock bag. Seal bag and place in refrigerator for 2 hours.
4. Once the unit is preheated, then add steak pieces in crisper basket. Close hood to start cooking.
5. Serve and enjoy.

Nutritional Value (Amount per Serving):

- Calories 190
- Fat 8.1 g
- Carbohydrates 3.3 g
- Sugar 1.35 g
- Protein 25.05 g
- Cholesterol 68 mg

Honey Pork Chops

Preparation Time: 10 minutes
Cooking Time: 12 minutes
Serve: 4

Ingredients:

- 1 lb pork chops, boneless
- 1/4 cup mayonnaise
- 1/4 cup honey
- 2 tbsp BBQ sauce
- 1/4 cup brown mustard
- Pepper
- Salt

Directions:

1. Place crisper basket on the grill grate and close hood.
2. Press AIR CRISP button. Set temperature to 360 F and time for 12 minutes. Press START/STOP to begin preheating.
3. In a bowl, coat pork chops with mayonnaise, mustard, honey, BBQ sauce, pepper, and salt. Cover and place in refrigerator for 1 hour.
4. Once the unit is preheated, then place pork chops in crisper basket. Close hood to start cooking.
5. Serve and enjoy.

Nutritional Value (Amount per Serving):

- Calories 366
- Fat 17.87 g
- Carbohydrates 20.5 g
- Sugar 18.61 g
- Protein 30.94 g
- Cholesterol 95 mg

Steak Tips with Potatoes

Preparation Time: 10 minutes
Cooking Time: 20 minutes
Serve: 4

Ingredients:

- 1 lb steaks, cut into 1/2-inch pieces
- 1/2 lb potatoes, cut into 1/2-inch pieces
- 1/4 tsp red pepper flakes, crushed
- 1/2 tsp garlic powder
- 2 tbsp butter, melted
- Pepper
- Salt

Directions:

1. Place crisper basket on the grill grate and close hood.
2. Press AIR CRISP button. Set temperature to 400 F and time for 20 minutes. Press START/STOP to begin preheating.
3. Add potatoes into the boiling water and cook for 5 minutes. Drain well and set aside.
4. In a mixing bowl, toss steak pieces with melted butter, potatoes, garlic powder, red pepper flakes, pepper, and salt.
5. Once the unit is preheated, then add steak mixture in crisper basket. Close hood to start cooking.
6. Stir steak mixture halfway through.
7. Serve and enjoy.

Nutritional Value (Amount per Serving):

- Calories 331
- Fat 17.34 g
- Carbohydrates 11.53 g
- Sugar 1.17 g
- Protein 33.11 g
- Cholesterol 101 mg

Meatballs

Preparation Time: 10 minutes
Cooking Time: 12 minutes
Serve: 16

Ingredients:

- 1 egg
- 1 ½ lbs ground beef
- 1/2 tsp onion powder
- 2 tbsp milk
- 1/3 cup breadcrumbs
- 1/2 tsp Italian seasoning
- 1 tbsp parmesan cheese, grated
- 2 tbsp parsley, chopped
- Pepper
- Salt

Directions:

1. Place crisper basket on the grill grate and close hood.
2. Press AIR CRISP button. Set temperature to 400 F and time for 12 minutes. Press START/STOP to begin preheating.
3. In a mixing bowl, mix meat and remaining ingredients until well combined.
4. Make small balls from the meat mixture.
5. Once the unit is preheated, then place meatballs in crisper basket. Close hood to start cooking.
6. Serve and enjoy.

Nutritional Value (Amount per Serving):

- Calories 120
- Fat 7.64 g
- Carbohydrates 0.6 g
- Sugar 0.3 g
- Protein 11.53 g
- Cholesterol 77 mg

Teriyaki Pork Chops

Preparation Time: 10 minutes
Cooking Time: 16 minutes
Serve: 4

Ingredients:

- 4 pork chops
- 2 tbsp horseradish sauce
- 1/4 tsp cinnamon
- 1/3 cup Teriyaki sauce

Directions:

1. Place crisper basket on the grill grate and close hood.
2. Press AIR CRISP button. Set temperature to 400 F and time for 16 minutes. Press START/STOP to begin preheating.
3. Add pork chops and remaining ingredients into the zip-lock bag. Seal bag and place in refrigerator for 30 minutes.
4. Once the unit is preheated, then place marinated pork chops in crisper basket. Close hood to start cooking.
5. Turn pork chops halfway through.
6. Serve and enjoy.

Nutritional Value (Amount per Serving):

- Calories 364
- Fat 18.84 g
- Carbohydrates 4.22 g
- Sugar 3.62 g
- Protein 41.73 g
- Cholesterol 137 mg

Juicy Steak Bites

Preparation Time: 10 minutes
Cooking Time: 10 minutes
Serve: 4

Ingredients:

- 1 1/4 lbs sirloin steak, cut into 1-inch pieces
- 1 lime juice
- 1 garlic clove, minced
- 1 tbsp butter, melted
- 1 lime zest, grated
- 2 tsp chili powder
- 1/2 jalapeno pepper, minced
- Pepper
- Salt

Directions:

1. Place crisper basket on the grill grate and close hood.
2. Press AIR CRISP button. Set temperature to 400 F and time for 10 minutes. Press START/STOP to begin preheating.
3. In a bowl, toss steak pieces with remaining ingredients until well coated.
4. Once the unit is preheated, then add steak mixture in crisper basket. Close hood to start cooking.
5. Serve and enjoy.

Nutritional Value (Amount per Serving):

- Calories 309
- Fat 18.9 g
- Carbohydrates 3.95 g
- Sugar 1.12 g
- Protein 29.91 g
- Cholesterol 110 mg

CHAPTER 4: SEAFOOD

Grill Fish Skewers

Preparation Time: 10 minutes
Cooking Time: 10 minutes
Serve: 4

Ingredients:

- 1 1/2 lbs white fish fillets, cut into 2-inch cubes
- 2 bell peppers, cut into 1-inch pieces
- 1 tbsp garlic, minced
- 4 tbsp olive oil
- 1/2 tsp ground cumin
- 1/2 tsp paprika
- 2 tbsp fresh lemon juice
- 1/4 tsp pepper
- 1 tsp kosher salt

Directions:

1. Plug thermometer into the ninja foodi smart XL pro grill unit.
2. Insert grill grate in the unit and close hood.
3. Press GRILL. Set temperature to MED. Press PRESET, then select FISH. Press START/STOP to begin preheating.
4. Add fish cubes and remaining ingredients into the zip-lock bag. Seal bag and place in refrigerator for 1 hour.
5. Insert the thermometer into the center of one of the fish cubes.
6. Thread marinated fish cubes and bell pepper pieces onto the skewers.
7. Once the unit is preheated, place fish skewers on the grill grate. Close hood.
8. When beeps and display indicate FLIP then flip fish skewers. Close hood to continue cooking.
9. Serve and enjoy.

Nutritional Value (Amount per Serving):

- Calories 286
- Fat 14.99 g
- Carbohydrates 39.17 g
- Sugar 17 g
- Protein 5.9 g
- Cholesterol 0 mg

Lemon Butter Cod

Preparation Time: 10 minutes
Cooking Time: 10 minutes
Serve: 4

Ingredients:

- 1 lb cod fillets, boneless & skinless
- 1/4 cup butter, melted
- 1/4 tsp dried parsley
- 1 lemon juice
- Pepper
- Salt

Directions:

1. Plug thermometer into the ninja foodi smart XL pro grill unit.
2. Insert grill grate in the unit and close hood.
3. Press GRILL. Set temperature to MED. Press PRESET, then select FISH. Press START/STOP to begin preheating.
4. In a small bowl, mix butter, parsley, lemon juice, pepper, and salt.
5. Brush fish fillets with butter mixture.
6. Insert the thermometer into the center of one of the fish fillets.
7. Once the unit is preheated, place fish fillets on the grill grate. Close hood.
8. When beeps and display indicate FLIP then flip fish fillets. Close hood to continue cooking.
9. Serve and enjoy.

Nutritional Value (Amount per Serving):

- Calories 259
- Fat 16.17 g
- Carbohydrates 1.91 g
- Sugar 0.89 g
- Protein 25.78 g
- Cholesterol 102 mg

Spicy Fish Fillets

Preparation Time: 10 minutes
Cooking Time: 10 minutes
Serve: 4

Ingredients:

- 2 lbs rockfish fillets
- 1/4 tsp cayenne
- 1 tbsp fresh lemon juice
- 2 tbsp fresh basil, chopped
- 1 tbsp garlic, minced
- 4 tbsp butter
- 3 tbsp olive oil

Directions:

1. Plug thermometer into the ninja foodi smart XL pro grill unit.
2. Insert grill grate in the unit and close hood.
3. Press GRILL. Set temperature to MED. Press PRESET, then select FISH. Press START/STOP to begin preheating.
4. Add fish fillets, lemon juice, and oil into the bowl and mix well. Cover and place in refrigerator for 30 minutes.
5. Insert the thermometer into the center of one of the fish fillets.
6. Once the unit is preheated, place marinated fish fillets on the grill grate. Close hood.
7. When beeps and display indicate FLIP then flip fish fillets. Close hood to continue cooking.
8. Melt butter in a small pan over low heat.
9. Add basil, garlic, cayenne, and pepper and stir well.
10. Drizzle butter mixture over fish fillets and serve.

Nutritional Value (Amount per Serving):

- Calories 400
- Fat 24.73 g
- Carbohydrates 1.08 g
- Sugar 0.14 g
- Protein 41.97 g
- Cholesterol 144 mg

Easy Grilled Tilapia

Preparation Time: 10 minutes
Cooking Time: 5 minutes
Serve: 4

Ingredients:

- 1 lb tilapia fillets
- 1 1/2 tbsp olive oil
- 1/2 tsp pepper
- 1 1/2 tbsp paprika
- 1 garlic clove, minced
- 1/2 tsp sea salt

Directions:

1. Plug thermometer into the ninja foodi smart XL pro grill unit.
2. Insert grill grate in the unit and close hood.
3. Press GRILL. Set temperature to MED. Press PRESET, then select FISH. Press START/STOP to begin preheating.
4. In a small bowl, mix together oil, garlic, paprika, pepper, and salt.
5. Brush fish fillets with oil mixture.
6. Insert the thermometer into the center of one of the fish fillets.
7. Once the unit is preheated, place fish fillets on the grill grate. Close hood.
8. When beeps and display indicate FLIP then flip fish fillets. Close hood to continue cooking.
9. Serve and enjoy.

Nutritional Value (Amount per Serving):

- Calories 164
- Fat 7.35 g
- Carbohydrates 2.16 g
- Sugar 0.56 g
- Protein 23.29 g
- Cholesterol 57 mg

Tasty Swordfish

Preparation Time: 10 minutes
Cooking Time: 10 minutes
Serve: 4

Ingredients:

- 4 swordfish steaks
- 1 tsp lemon zest
- 1 1/2 tbsp soy sauce
- 1 1/2 tbsp honey
- 1/4 cup olive oil
- 3/4 tsp garlic, minced
- 2 tsp thyme
- 2 tsp parsley, chopped
- 1/4 tsp pepper
- 1/2 tsp kosher salt

Directions:

1. Plug thermometer into the ninja foodi smart XL pro grill unit.
2. Insert grill grate in the unit and close hood.
3. Press GRILL. Set temperature to MED. Press PRESET, then select FISH. Press START/STOP to begin preheating.
4. Add swordfish steaks and remaining ingredients into the zip-lock bag. Seal bag and place in the refrigerator for 8 hours.
5. Insert the thermometer into the center of one of the fish fillets.
6. Once the unit is preheated, place fish fillets on the grill grate. Close hood.
7. When beeps and display indicate FLIP then flip fish fillets. Close hood to continue cooking.
8. Serve and enjoy.

Nutritional Value (Amount per Serving):

- Calories 657
- Fat 47.33 g
- Carbohydrates 8.64 g
- Sugar 7.81 g
- Protein 46.96 g
- Cholesterol 181 mg

Garlic Pepper Salmon

Preparation Time: 10 minutes
Cooking Time: 15 minutes
Serve: 4

Ingredients:

- 4 salmon fillets
- 1 1/2 tbsp ground mixed peppercorns
- 2 garlic cloves, minced
- 1/2 tbsp orange juice
- 1 tbsp olive oil
- 2 tsp honey
- 1/4 cup soy sauce

Directions:

1. Place crisper basket on the grill grate and close hood.
2. Press AIR CRISP button. Set temperature to 350 F and time for 15 minutes. Press START/STOP to begin preheating.
3. Add honey, garlic, soy sauce, orange juice, and salmon fillets into the zip-lock bag. Seal bag and place in refrigerator for 30 minutes.
4. Remove salmon fillets from marinade and pat dry.
5. Rub salmon fillets with oil and coat with peppercorns.
6. Once the unit is preheated, then place salmon fillets in crisper basket. Close hood to start cooking.
7. Serve and enjoy.

Nutritional Value (Amount per Serving):

- Calories 149
- Fat 9.12 g
- Carbohydrates 7.59 g
- Sugar 6.14 g
- Protein 9.19 g
- Cholesterol 26 mg

Salmon Patties

Preparation Time: 10 minutes
Cooking Time: 8 minutes
Serve: 6

Ingredients:

- 1 egg
- 14 oz can salmon, drained & minced
- 1/4 cup fresh coriander, chopped
- 1 tsp paprika
- 1/4 cup green onion, minced
- Salt

Directions:

1. Place crisper basket on the grill grate and close hood.
2. Press AIR CRISP button. Set temperature to 360 F and time for 8 minutes. Press START/STOP to begin preheating.
3. In a bowl, mix salmon, egg, paprika, green onion, coriander, and salt until well combined.
4. Make patties from the salmon mixture.
5. Once the unit is preheated, then place salmon patties in crisper basket. Close hood to start cooking.
6. Turn patties halfway through.
7. Serve and enjoy.

Nutritional Value (Amount per Serving):

- Calories 125
- Fat 6.24 g
- Carbohydrates 0.57 g
- Sugar 0.27 g
- Protein 15.24 g
- Cholesterol 147 mg

Crab Patties

Preparation Time: 10 minutes
Cooking Time: 10 minutes
Serve: 4

Ingredients:

- 8 oz crab meat
- 2 tbsp butter, melted
- 1/2 tsp old bay seasoning
- 1 green onion, sliced
- 2 tbsp parsley, chopped
- 2 tsp Dijon mustard
- 1 tbsp mayonnaise
- 1 egg, lightly beaten
- 1/4 cup almond flour
- Pepper
- salt

Directions:

1. Place crisper basket on the grill grate and close hood.
2. Press AIR CRISP button. Set temperature to 350 F and time for 10 minutes. Press START/STOP to begin preheating.
3. In a mixing bowl, add crab meat and remaining ingredients and mix until well combined.
4. Make patties from the meat mixture.
5. Once the unit is preheated, then place patties in crisper basket. Close hood to start cooking.
6. Serve and enjoy.

Nutritional Value (Amount per Serving):

- Calories 285
- Fat 11.29 g
- Carbohydrates 24.52 g
- Sugar 1.51 g
- Protein 24.7 g
- Cholesterol 170 mg

Thai White Fish Fillet

Preparation Time: 10 minutes
Cooking Time: 10 minutes
Serve: 2

Ingredients:

- 2 white fish fillets
- 1 tbsp garlic, minced
- 1 tbsp oyster sauce
- 1 tsp soy sauce
- 2 tsp fish sauce
- 1/2 tbsp lime juice
- 1 tbsp brown sugar

Directions:

1. Place crisper basket on the grill grate and close hood.
2. Press AIR CRISP button. Set temperature to 400 F and time for 10 minutes. Press START/STOP to begin preheating.
3. In a small bowl, mix together soy sauce, lime juice, fish sauce, garlic, oyster sauce, and brown sugar.
4. Brush fish fillets with soy sauce mixture.
5. Once the unit is preheated, then place fish fillets in crisper basket. Close hood to start cooking.
6. Serve and enjoy.

Nutritional Value (Amount per Serving):

- Calories 211
- Fat 11.13 g
- Carbohydrates 5.16 g
- Sugar 2.39 g
- Protein 21.6 g
- Cholesterol 56 mg

Blackened Tilapia

Preparation Time: 10 minutes
Cooking Time: 8 minutes
Serve: 4

Ingredients:

- 4 tilapia fillets
- 1 tsp garlic powder
- 1/4 tsp cayenne
- 1/2 tsp cumin
- 1 tbsp olive oil
- 1 tsp dried oregano
- 2 tsp brown sugar
- 2 tbsp paprika
- Salt

Directions:

1. Place crisper basket on the grill grate and close hood.
2. Press AIR CRISP button. Set temperature to 400 F and time for 8 minutes. Press START/STOP to begin preheating.
3. In a small bowl, mix cayenne, oregano, paprika, garlic powder, cumin, brown sugar, and oil.
4. Brush fish fillets with oil and rub with spice mixture.
5. Once the unit is preheated, then place fish fillets in crisper basket. Close hood to start cooking.
6. Serve and enjoy.
7. Turn fish fillets halfway through.
8. Serve and enjoy.

Nutritional Value (Amount per Serving):

- Calories 164
- Fat 5.88 g
- Carbohydrates 5.02 g
- Sugar 2.63 g
- Protein 23.99g
- Cholesterol 58 mg

Marinated Fish Bites

Preparation Time: 10 minutes
Cooking Time: 9 minutes
Serve: 2

Ingredients:

- 2 tilapia fillets, diced
- 2 tbsp honey
- 1 tbsp lemon juice
- 3 tbsp soy sauce
- 3 tbsp olive oil
- 1 tbsp sesame seeds
- 1/4 tsp ginger powder
- 1/2 tsp onion powder
- 1 tsp garlic powder

Directions:

1. Place crisper basket on the grill grate and close hood.
2. Press AIR CRISP button. Set temperature to 375 F and time for 9 minutes. Press START/STOP to begin preheating.
3. Add fish pieces and remaining ingredients into the bowl and mix well. Cover and place in refrigerator for 30 minutes.
4. Once the unit is preheated, then place marinated fish pieces in crisper basket. Close hood to start cooking.
5. Serve and enjoy.

Nutritional Value (Amount per Serving):

- Calories 458
- Fat 29.03 g
- Carbohydrates 25.89 g
- Sugar 22.15 g
- Protein 26.23 g
- Cholesterol 58 mg

Spicy Crab Patties

Preparation Time: 10 minutes
Cooking Time: 10 minutes
Serve: 4

Ingredients:

- 1 egg
- 8 oz lump crab meat
- 1/2 lemon juice
- 1/4 cup mayonnaise
- 1/4 cup green bell peppers, diced
- 1/4 cup red bell peppers, diced
- 1/3 cup breadcrumbs
- 1 tbsp old bay seasoning
- Pepper
- Salt

Directions:

1. Place crisper basket on the grill grate and close hood.
2. Press AIR CRISP button. Set temperature to 370 F and time for 10 minutes. Press START/STOP to begin preheating.
3. In a bowl, mix crab meat, egg, bell peppers, breadcrumbs, lemon juice, mayonnaise, old bay seasoning, pepper, and salt until well combined.
4. Make patties from crab meat mixture.
5. Once the unit is preheated, then place patties in crisper basket. Close hood to start cooking.
6. Serve and enjoy.
7. Turn patties halfway through.
8. Serve and enjoy.

Nutritional Value (Amount per Serving):

- Calories 268
- Fat 8.95 g
- Carbohydrates 24.79 g
- Sugar 1.3 g
- Protein 25.14 g
- Cholesterol 155 mg

Air Fry Mahi Mahi

Preparation Time: 10 minutes
Cooking Time: 12 minutes
Serve: 2

Ingredients:

- 2 mahi-mahi fillets
- 2 tbsp butter, melted
- 2 tbsp parmesan cheese, grated
- Pepper
- Salt

Directions:

1. Place crisper basket on the grill grate and close hood.
2. Press AIR CRISP button. Set temperature to 350 F and time for 12 minutes. Press START/STOP to begin preheating.
3. In a small bowl, mix butter, cheese, pepper, and salt.
4. Brush fish fillets with butter mixture.
5. Once the unit is preheated, then place fish fillets in crisper basket. Close hood to start cooking.
6. Serve and enjoy.

Nutritional Value (Amount per Serving):

- Calories 378
- Fat 28.25 g
- Carbohydrates 10.48 g
- Sugar 1.84 g
- Protein 21.54 g
- Cholesterol 35 mg

Healthy Tuna Steaks

Preparation Time: 10 minutes
Cooking Time: 10 minutes
Serve: 2

Ingredients:

- 1 lb tuna steaks
- 6 garlic cloves, minced
- 1 tsp thyme
- 1/4 cup olive oil
- 1 tbsp garlic powder
- Pepper
- Salt

Directions:

1. Place crisper basket on the grill grate and close hood.
2. Press AIR CRISP button. Set temperature to 400 F and time for 10 minutes. Press START/STOP to begin preheating.
3. In a bowl, coat tuna steaks with oil, garlic, garlic powder, thyme, pepper, and salt. Cover and set aside for 20 minutes.
4. Once the unit is preheated, then place tuna steaks in crisper basket. Close hood to start cooking.
5. Serve and enjoy.

Nutritional Value (Amount per Serving):

- Calories 883
- Fat 67.25 g
- Carbohydrates 8.73 g
- Sugar 1.36 g
- Protein 58.71 g
- Cholesterol 222 mg

Asian Salmon Steaks

Preparation Time: 10 minutes
Cooking Time: 19 minutes
Serve: 2

Ingredients:

- 2 salmon steaks
- 2 tbsp sesame oil
- 3 tbsp Worcestershire sauce
- 3 tbsp garlic paste
- 2 tbsp rice vinegar
- Pepper
- Salt

Directions:

1. Place crisper basket on the grill grate and close hood.
2. Press AIR CRISP button. Set temperature to 400 F and time for 15 minutes. Press START/STOP to begin preheating.
3. In a bowl, mix salmon steak, oil, Worcestershire sauce, garlic paste, vinegar, pepper, and salt. Cover and place in refrigerator for 1 hour.
4. Once the unit is preheated, then place marinated salmon steaks in crisper basket. Close hood to start cooking.
5. Serve and enjoy.
6. Turn salmon steak and cook for 4 minutes more.
7. Serve and enjoy.

Nutritional Value (Amount per Serving):

- Calories 215
- Fat 15.74 g
- Carbohydrates 11.44 g
- Sugar 3.89 g
- Protein 7.11 g
- Cholesterol 19 mg

CHAPTER 5: SNACKS & SIDES

Marinated Tofu Bites

Preparation Time: 10 minutes
Cooking Time: 12 minutes
Serve: 4

Ingredients:

- 14 oz extra-firm tofu, cut into pieces
- 1/2 tsp sugar
- 2 tsp ginger, grated
- 2 tbsp fresh lime juice
- 2 tbsp soy sauce
- 2 tsp garlic, minced

Directions:

1. Place crisper basket on the grill grate and close hood.
2. Press AIR CRISP button. Set temperature to 400 F and time for 12 minutes. Press START/STOP to begin preheating.
3. In a bowl, mix tofu with lime juice, ginger, soy sauce, sugar, and garlic until well coated. Cover and place in refrigerator for 3 hours.
4. Once the unit is preheated, then place tofu pieces in crisper basket. Close hood to start cooking.
5. Turn tofu pieces halfway through.
6. Serve and enjoy.

Nutritional Value (Amount per Serving):

- Calories 119
- Fat 7.25 g
- Carbohydrates 5.57 g
- Sugar 2.51 g
- Protein 10.52 g
- Cholesterol 0 mg

Cinnamon Carrot Fries

Preparation Time: 10 minutes
Cooking Time: 12 minutes
Serve: 4

Ingredients:

- 1 lb carrots, cut into the shape of fries
- 1 tsp olive oil
- 1/2 tsp cinnamon
- 1 tsp maple syrup
- Salt

Directions:

1. Place crisper basket on the grill grate and close hood.
2. Press AIR CRISP button. Set temperature to 400 F and time for 12 minutes. Press START/STOP to begin preheating.
3. In a bowl, toss carrot with cinnamon, oil, maple syrup, and salt.
4. Once the unit is preheated, then add carrots in crisper basket. Close hood to start cooking.
5. Serve and enjoy.

Nutritional Value (Amount per Serving):

- Calories 55
- Fat 1.33 g
- Carbohydrates 10.69 g
- Sugar 4.92 g
- Protein 0.88 g
- Cholesterol 0 mg

Crispy Chickpeas

Preparation Time: 10 minutes
Cooking Time: 17 minutes
Serve: 4

Ingredients:

- 14 oz can chickpeas, rinsed, drained & pat dry
- 2 tsp lime zest, grated
- 2 tsp chili powder
- 2 tsp ground cumin
- ¼ tsp paprika
- 1 tsp salt

Directions:

1. Place crisper basket on the grill grate and close hood.
2. Press AIR CRISP button. Set temperature to 400 F and time for 17 minutes. Press START/STOP to begin preheating.
3. In a bowl, toss chickpeas with chili powder, paprika, cumin, lime zest, and salt.
4. Once the unit is preheated, then add chickpeas in crisper basket. Close hood to start cooking.
5. Stir chickpeas halfway through.
6. Serve and enjoy.

Nutritional Value (Amount per Serving):

- Calories 146
- Fat 2.9g
- Carbohydrates 24.12 g
- Sugar4.15 g
- Protein 7.39 g
- Cholesterol 0 mg

Air Fry Walnuts

Preparation Time: 10 minutes
Cooking Time: 10 minutes
Serve: 2

Ingredients:

- 1 cup walnuts halves
- 1/4 tsp white pepper powder
- 1/4 tsp cayenne
- 1/4 tsp ground cumin
- 2 tbsp sesame seeds
- 1/2 tbsp butter, melted
- 1 tbsp water
- 1/4 cup sugar
- 1/4 tsp salt

Directions:

1. Place crisper basket on the grill grate and close hood.
2. Press AIR CRISP button. Set temperature to 300 F and time for 10 minutes. Press START/STOP to begin preheating.
3. Add walnuts and remaining ingredients into the mixing bowl and toss until well coated.
4. Once the unit is preheated, then add walnuts in crisper basket. Close hood to start cooking.
5. Serve and enjoy.

Nutritional Value (Amount per Serving):

- Calories 389
- Fat 33.96 g
- Carbohydrates 19.16 g
- Sugar 13.34 g
- Protein 8.08 g
- Cholesterol 8 mg

Spinach Carrot Balls

Preparation Time: 10 minutes
Cooking Time: 10 minutes
Serve: 4

Ingredients:

- 1 egg
- 1/4 cup breadcrumbs
- 1/2 tsp garlic powder
- 1/2 onion, chopped
- 1 cup spinach, blanched & chopped
- 1 tbsp corn flour
- 1 tbsp nutritional yeast
- 1 tsp garlic, minced
- 1 carrot, peel & grated
- Pepper
- Salt

Directions:

1. Place crisper basket on the grill grate and close hood.
2. Press AIR CRISP button. Set temperature to 390 F and time for 10 minutes. Press START/STOP to begin preheating.
3. Add spinach and remaining ingredients into the mixing bowl and mix until well combined.
4. Make small balls from the spinach mixture.
5. Once the unit is preheated, then place spinach balls in crisper basket. Close hood to start cooking.
6. Serve and enjoy.

Nutritional Value (Amount per Serving):

- Calories 68
- Fat 2.63 g
- Carbohydrates 7.18 g
- Sugar 2.17 g
- Protein 4.29 g
- Cholesterol 155 mg

Zucchini Fritters

Preparation Time: 10 minutes
Cooking Time: 12 minutes
Serve: 4

Ingredients:

- 1 egg
- 2 zucchini, grated & squeezed
- 1 tbsp dill, chopped
- 1 tbsp garlic, minced
- 2 tbsp chives
- 1/4 cup onion, grated
- 2 oz feta cheese, crumbled
- 1/4 cup breadcrumbs
- 1/4 cup flour
- Pepper
- Salt

Directions:

1. Place crisper basket on the grill grate and close hood.
2. Press AIR CRISP button. Set temperature to 375 F and time for 12 minutes. Press START/STOP to begin preheating.
3. Add zucchini and remaining ingredients into the mixing bowl and mix until well combined.
4. Make small patties from the zucchini mixture.
5. Once the unit is preheated, then place zucchini patties in crisper basket. Close hood to start cooking.
6. Turn patties halfway through.
7. Serve and enjoy.

Nutritional Value (Amount per Serving):

- Calories 115
- Fat 5.82 g
- Carbohydrates 10.39g
- Sugar1.69 g
- Protein 5.97 g
- Cholesterol 167 mg

Sweet Potato Wedges

Preparation Time: 10 minutes
Cooking Time: 20 minutes
Serve: 2

Ingredients:

- 1 sweet potato, cut into wedges
- 1/2 tsp garlic powder
- 1/2 tsp paprika
- 1/8 tsp cayenne
- 1 tbsp olive oil
- ¼ tsp chili powder
- Pepper
- Salt

Directions:

1. Place crisper basket on the grill grate and close hood.
2. Press AIR CRISP button. Set temperature to 400 F and time for 20 minutes. Press START/STOP to begin preheating.
3. In a bowl, toss sweet potato wedges with oil, paprika, garlic powder, cayenne, pepper, and salt.
4. Once the unit is preheated, then add sweet potato wedges in crisper basket. Close hood to start cooking.
5. Turn wedges halfway through.
6. Serve and enjoy.

Nutritional Value (Amount per Serving):

- Calories 82
- Fat 7.03 g
- Carbohydrates 4.81 g
- Sugar 1.26 g
- Protein 1.16 g
- Cholesterol 0 mg

Zucchini Cheese Balls

Preparation Time: 10 minutes
Cooking Time: 10 minutes
Serve: 4

Ingredients:

- 2 eggs, lightly beaten
- 1 medium zucchini, grated & squeezed
- 1 1/2 cups pepper jack cheese, shredded
- 1/3 cup breadcrumbs
- 1/4 tsp onion powder
- 1/2 tsp paprika
- 1 tsp garlic powder
- Pepper
- Salt

Directions:

1. Place crisper basket on the grill grate and close hood.
2. Press AIR CRISP button. Set temperature to 380 F and time for 10 minutes. Press START/STOP to begin preheating.
3. In a bowl, mix grated zucchini and remaining ingredients until well combined.
4. Make small balls from the zucchini mixture.
5. Once the unit is preheated, then place zucchini balls in crisper basket. Close hood to start cooking.
6. Serve and enjoy.

Nutritional Value (Amount per Serving):

- Calories 258
- Fat 19. 89 g
- Carbohydrates 2.84g
- Sugar 1.21 g
- Protein 17.09 g
- Cholesterol 353 mg

Italian Cauliflower Balls

Preparation Time: 10 minutes
Cooking Time: 10 minutes
Serve: 6

Ingredients:

- 2 eggs, lightly beaten
- 16 oz cauliflower rice, steam & squeezed
- 6 tbsp breadcrumbs
- 2 tbsp parmesan cheese, grated
- 1 1/2 cups mozzarella cheese, shredded
- 1 tsp dried parsley
- 1 tsp garlic powder
- 1/2 tsp onion powder
- Pepper
- Salt

Directions:

1. Place crisper basket on the grill grate and close hood.
2. Press AIR CRISP button. Set temperature to 380 F and time for 10 minutes. Press START/STOP to begin preheating.
3. In a bowl, mix cauliflower rice and the remaining ingredients until well combined.
4. Make small balls from the cauliflower mixture.
5. Once the unit is preheated, then place cauliflower balls in crisper basket. Close hood to start cooking.
6. Serve and enjoy.

Nutritional Value (Amount per Serving):

- Calories 131
- Fat 4.43 g
- Carbohydrates 9.75 g
- Sugar 5.04 g
- Protein 12.89 g
- Cholesterol 213 mg

Parmesan Broccoli

Preparation Time: 10 minutes
Cooking Time: 10 minutes
Serve: 4

Ingredients:

- 1 lb broccoli florets
- 1 lemon zest, grated
- 1 tsp onion powder
- 4 tbsp parmesan cheese, grated
- 2 tbsp olive oil
- 1 lemon juice
- 1 tsp garlic powder
- Pepper
- Salt

Directions:

1. Place crisper basket on the grill grate and close hood.
2. Press AIR CRISP button. Set temperature to 400 F and time for 10 minutes. Press START/STOP to begin preheating.
3. In a bowl, toss broccoli florets with oil, onion powder, garlic powder, pepper, and salt.
4. Once the unit is preheated, then add broccoli in crisper basket. Close hood to start cooking.
5. Transfer broccoli onto a plate and top with lemon juice, grated cheese, and lemon zest.
6. Serve and enjoy.

Nutritional Value (Amount per Serving):

- Calories 120
- Fat 8.79 g
- Carbohydrates 7.69 g
- Sugar 1.67 g
- Protein 5.52 g
- Cholesterol 4 mg

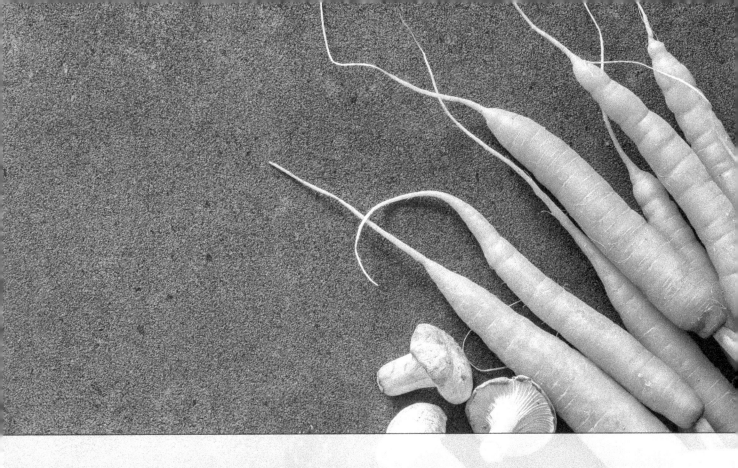

CHAPTER 6: VEGETABLES

Crispy Potatoes

Preparation Time: 10 minutes
Cooking Time: 20 minutes
Serve: 6

Ingredients:

- 2 lbs baby potatoes, clean & cut in half
- 2 tbsp olive oil
- 1 tbsp garlic, minced
- 1 tbsp fresh rosemary, minced
- Pepper
- Salt

Directions:

1. Place crisper basket on the grill grate and close hood.
2. Press AIR CRISP button. Set temperature to 400 F and time for 20 minutes. Press START/STOP to begin preheating.
3. In a bowl, toss potatoes with rosemary, oil, garlic, salt, and pepper until well coated.
4. Once the unit is preheated, then add potatoes in crisper basket. Close hood to start cooking.
5. Stir potatoes halfway through.
6. Serve and enjoy.

Nutritional Value (Amount per Serving):

- Calories 162
- Fat 4.67 g
- Carbohydrates 27.65 g
- Sugar 1.58 g
- Protein 3.3 g
- Cholesterol 0 mg

Crispy Cauliflower

Preparation Time: 10 minutes
Cooking Time: 6 minutes
Serve: 2

Ingredients:

- 2 cups cauliflower florets
- 1/2 tbsp canola oil
- 1/8 tsp ground nutmeg
- Pepper
- Salt

Directions:

1. Place crisper basket on the grill grate and close hood.
2. Press AIR CRISP button. Set temperature to 400 F and time for 6 minutes. Press START/STOP to begin preheating.
3. In a bowl, toss cauliflower florets with oil, nutmeg, pepper, and salt.
4. Once the unit is preheated, then add cauliflower florets in crisper basket. Close hood to start cooking.
5. Serve and enjoy.

Nutritional Value (Amount per Serving):

- Calories 67
- Fat 3.9 g
- Carbohydrates 7.52 g
- Sugar 3.2 g
- Protein 2.51 g
- Cholesterol 0 mg

Balsamic Vegetables

Preparation Time: 10 minutes
Cooking Time: 15 minutes
Serve: 6

Ingredients:

- 1 cup mushrooms, sliced
- 2 eggplants, cut into cubes
- 1/2 onion, diced
- 2 tbsp balsamic vinegar
- 12 grape tomatoes
- 2 tbsp olive oil
- 1 yellow squash, cut into cubes
- 1 zucchini, cut into cubes
- Pepper
- Salt

Directions:

1. Place crisper basket on the grill grate and close hood.
2. Press AIR CRISP button. Set temperature to 390 F and time for 15 minutes. Press START/STOP to begin preheating.
3. In a bowl, toss vegetables with oil, vinegar, pepper, and salt.
4. Once the unit is preheated, then add vegetables in crisper basket. Close hood to start cooking.
5. Stir vegetables halfway through.
6. Serve and enjoy.

Nutritional Value (Amount per Serving):

- Calories 116
- Fat 5.06 g
- Carbohydrates 17.52 g
- Sugar 11.2 g
- Protein 2.73 g
- Cholesterol 0 mg

BBQ Green Beans

Preparation Time: 10 minutes
Cooking Time: 15 minutes
Serve: 4

Ingredients:

- 1 lb green beans, trimmed
- 1/3 cup BBQ sauce
- 2 tsp sesame seeds, toasted
- 1/2 tsp ground black pepper

Directions:

1. Place crisper basket on the grill grate and close hood.
2. Press AIR CRISP button. Set temperature to 400 F and time for 15 minutes. Press START/STOP to begin preheating.
3. In a mixing bowl, toss green beans with BBQ sauce and pepper.
4. Once the unit is preheated, then add green beans in crisper basket. Close hood to start cooking.
5. Stir green beans halfway through.
6. Sprinkle with sesame seeds and serve.

Nutritional Value (Amount per Serving):

- Calories 42
- Fat 1.4 g
- Carbohydrates 7.03 g
- Sugar 2.02 g
- Protein 1.99 g
- Cholesterol 0 mg

Crispy Brussels Sprouts

Preparation Time: 10 minutes
Cooking Time: 10 minutes
Serve: 5

Ingredients:

- 2 cups Brussels sprouts, cut in half
- 1 tbsp olive oil
- 1/2 cup onions, sliced
- 1 tbsp balsamic vinegar
- Pepper
- Salt

Directions:

1. Place crisper basket on the grill grate and close hood.
2. Press AIR CRISP button. Set temperature to 350 F and time for 10 minutes. Press START/STOP to begin preheating.
3. Add Brussels sprouts, vinegar, onion, oil, pepper, and salt into the bowl and toss well.
4. Once the unit is preheated, then add Brussels sprout mixture in crisper basket. Close hood to start cooking. Stir halfway through.
5. Serve and enjoy.

Nutritional Value (Amount per Serving):

- Calories 50
- Fat 2.84 g
- Carbohydrates 5.62 g
- Sugar 2.2 g
- Protein 1.51 g
- Cholesterol 0 mg

Herb Butter Radishes

Preparation Time: 10 minutes
Cooking Time: 10 minutes
Serve: 4

Ingredients:

- 1 lb radishes, cut into quarters
- 1/4 tsp dried oregano
- 2 tbsp butter, melted
- 1/2 tsp dried parsley
- 1/2 tsp garlic powder
- Pepper
- Salt

Directions:

1. Place crisper basket on the grill grate and close hood.
2. Press AIR CRISP button. Set temperature to 350 F and time for 10 minutes. Press START/STOP to begin preheating.
3. In a bowl, toss radishes with butter, oregano, pepper, garlic powder, dried parsley, and salt.
4. Once the unit is preheated, then add radishes in crisper basket. Close hood to start cooking. Stir halfway through.
5. Serve and enjoy.

Nutritional Value (Amount per Serving):

- Calories 77
- Fat 5.9 g
- Carbohydrates 6.07 g
- Sugar 3.43 g
- Protein 1.04 g
- Cholesterol 15 mg

Eggplant Bites

Preparation Time: 10 minutes
Cooking Time: 15 minutes
Serve: 4

Ingredients:

- 1 1/2 lbs eggplant, cut into 1/2-inch pieces
- 1 tsp garlic powder
- 2 tbsp vegetable broth
- 1/4 tsp dried thyme
- 1/2 tsp dried oregano
- 1 tsp paprika
- Pepper
- Salt

Directions:

1. Place crisper basket on the grill grate and close hood.
2. Press AIR CRISP button. Set temperature to 380 F and time for 15 minutes. Press START/STOP to begin preheating.
3. In a bowl, toss eggplant with thyme, garlic powder, oregano, paprika, vegetable broth, pepper, and salt.
4. Once the unit is preheated, then add eggplant pieces in crisper basket. Close hood to start cooking. Stir halfway through.
5. Serve and enjoy.

Nutritional Value (Amount per Serving):

- Calories 52
- Fat 0.41 g
- Carbohydrates 12.13 g
- Sugar 6.72 g
- Protein 2.12 g
- Cholesterol 0 mg

Air Fry Artichoke Hearts

Preparation Time: 10 minutes
Cooking Time: 8 minutes
Serve: 4

Ingredients:

- 14 oz can artichoke hearts, drained & quartered
- 1 tbsp olive oil
- 2 tsp parmesan cheese, grated
- 1/8 tsp garlic powder
- 1/4 tsp Italian seasoning
- Pepper
- Salt

Directions:

1. Place crisper basket on the grill grate and close hood.
2. Press AIR CRISP button. Set temperature to 390 F and time for 8 minutes. Press START/STOP to begin preheating.
3. In a bowl, toss artichoke with oil, parmesan cheese, garlic powder, Italian seasoning, pepper, and salt.
4. Once the unit is preheated, then add artichoke in crisper basket. Close hood to start cooking. Stir halfway through.
5. Serve and enjoy.

Nutritional Value (Amount per Serving):

- Calories 92
- Fat 4.03 g
- Carbohydrates 13.24 g
- Sugar 1.58 g
- Protein 3.42 g
- Cholesterol 1 mg

Garlic Snow Peas

Preparation Time: 10 minutes
Cooking Time: 8 minutes
Serve: 2

Ingredients:

- 3 cups snow peas
- 2 bacon slices, chopped
- 4 garlic cloves, sliced
- Pepper
- Salt

Directions:

1. Place crisper basket on the grill grate and close hood.
2. Press AIR CRISP button. Set temperature to 320 F and time for 8 minutes. Press START/STOP to begin preheating.
3. In a bowl, mix snow peas, garlic, bacon, pepper, and salt.
4. Once the unit is preheated, then add snow peas mixture in crisper basket. Close hood to start cooking. Stir halfway through.
5. Serve and enjoy.

Nutritional Value (Amount per Serving):

- Calories 126
- Fat 10.3 g
- Carbohydrates 4.71 g
- Sugar 1.63 g
- Protein 4.23 g
- Cholesterol 0 mg

Roasted Mix Veggies

Preparation Time: 10 minutes
Cooking Time: 12 minutes
Serve: 4

Ingredients:

- 1 cup broccoli florets
- 1 red bell pepper, diced
- 1 tbsp olive oil
- 1/2 tsp garlic powder
- 1/4 onion, sliced
- 1 zucchini, sliced
- 2 yellow squash, sliced
- Pepper
- Salt

Directions:

1. Place crisper basket on the grill grate and close hood.
2. Press AIR CRISP button. Set temperature to 400 F and time for 12 minutes. Press START/STOP to begin preheating.
3. In a bowl, toss vegetables with oil, garlic powder, pepper, and salt.
4. Once the unit is preheated, then add vegetables in crisper basket. Close hood to start cooking. Stir halfway through.
5. Serve and enjoy.

Nutritional Value (Amount per Serving):

- Calories44
- Fat 3.5 g
- Carbohydrates 3.03 g
- Sugar 1.32 g
- Protein 0.95 g
- Cholesterol 0 mg

CHAPTER 7: DESSERTS

Lemon Brownies

Preparation Time: 10 minutes
Cooking Time: 20 minutes
Serve: 16

Ingredients:

- 2 eggs
- 1 tbsp fresh lemon juice
- ½ lemon zest
- ½ tsp baking powder
- ¾ cup all-purpose flour
- ¾ cup sugar
- ½ cup butter, softened

Directions:

1. Insert grill grate in the unit and close hood.
2. Press BAKE button. Set temperature to 350 F and time for 20 minutes. Press START/STOP to begin preheating.
3. In a large bowl, beat sugar, butter, and lemon zest until fluffy.
4. Add eggs, lemon juice, and flour and mix until combined.
5. Pour batter into the greased baking dish.
6. Once the unit is preheated, then place the baking dish on the grill grate. Close hood to start cooking.
7. Slice and serve.

Nutritional Value (Amount per Serving):

- Calories 107
- Fat 7.02 g
- Carbohydrates 9.52 g
- Sugar 4.75 g
- Protein 1.8 g
- Cholesterol 93 mg

Butter Cake

Preparation Time: 10 minutes
Cooking Time: 30 minutes
Serve: 8

Ingredients:

- 1 egg, beaten
- 1/2 cup butter, softened
- 1 cup all-purpose flour
- 3/4 cup sugar
- 1/2 tsp vanilla

Directions:

1. Insert grill grate in the unit and close hood.
2. Press BAKE button. Set temperature to 350 F and time for 30 minutes. Press START/STOP to begin preheating.
3. In a mixing bowl, mix together sugar and butter.
4. Add egg, flour, and vanilla and mix until combined.
5. Pour batter into the greased baking dish.
6. Once the unit is preheated, then place the baking dish on the grill grate. Close hood to start cooking.
7. Slice and serve.

Nutritional Value (Amount per Serving):

- Calories 212
- Fat 12.87 g
- Carbohydrates 21.45 g
- Sugar 9.33 g
- Protein 2.86 g
- Cholesterol 108 mg

Almond Butter Brownies

Preparation Time: 10 minutes
Cooking Time: 20 minutes
Serve: 4

Ingredients:

- 1 scoop protein powder
- 1/2 cup almond butter, melted
- 2 tbsp cocoa powder
- 1 cup bananas, overripe

Directions:

1. Insert grill grate in the unit and close hood.
2. Press BAKE button. Set temperature to 350 F and time for 20 minutes. Press START/STOP to begin preheating.
3. Add all ingredients into the blender and blend until smooth.
4. Pour batter into the greased baking dish.
5. Once the unit is preheated, then place the baking dish on the grill grate. Close hood to start cooking.
6. Slice and serve.

Nutritional Value (Amount per Serving):

- Calories 328
- Fat 18.78 g
- Carbohydrates 32.78 g
- Protein 14.26 g
- Sugars 16.33 g
- Cholesterol 0 mg

Baked Donuts

Preparation Time: 10 minutes
Cooking Time: 15 minutes
Serve: 6

Ingredients:

- 2 eggs
- 1 cup almond flour
- 1/4 tsp baking soda
- 1 1/2 tsp vanilla
- 3 tbsp maple syrup

Directions:

1. Insert grill grate in the unit and close hood.
2. Press BAKE button. Set temperature to 320 F and time for 15 minutes. Press START/STOP to begin preheating.
3. In a large bowl, add all ingredients and mix well until smooth.
4. Pour batter into the greased donut pan.
5. Once the unit is preheated, then place the donut pan on the grill grate. Close hood to start cooking.
6. Serve and enjoy.

Nutritional Value (Amount per Serving):

- Calories 73
- Fat 3.32 g
- Carbohydrates 7.22 g
- Protein 3.04 g
- Sugars 6.4 g
- Cholesterol 206 mg

Moist Banana Cake

Preparation Time: 10 minutes
Cooking Time: 40 minutes
Serve: 8

Ingredients:

- 2 large eggs, beaten
- 2 cups all-purpose flour
- 2 bananas, mashed
- 1 tsp baking soda
- 1 1/2 cup sugar, granulated
- 1 tsp vanilla
- 1/2 cup butter
- 1 cup milk
- 1 tsp baking powder

Directions:

1. Insert grill grate in the unit and close hood.
2. Press BAKE button. Set temperature to 350 F and time for 40 minutes. Press START/STOP to begin preheating.
3. In a bowl, beat together sugar and butter until creamy. Add in eggs and mix well.
4. Add milk, baking powder, vanilla, baking soda, flour, and mashed bananas into the mixture and beat for 2 minutes. Mix well.
5. Pour batter into the greased baking dish.
6. Once the unit is preheated, then place the baking dish on the grill grate. Close hood to start cooking.
7. Slice and serve.

Nutritional Value (Amount per Serving):

- Calories 409
- Fat 14.39 g
- Carbohydrates 66.60 g
- Protein 5.96 g
- Sugar 31.89 g
- Cholesterol 80 mg

CONCLUSION

The Ninja Foodi smart XL grill is one of the revolutionary cooking appliances that come from the Ninja Family. These 7 in 1 multifunctional cooking appliances not only grill your food but also roast, broil, bake, Air Crisp, and even dehydrate your favorite foods.

This cookbook contains healthy and delicious Ninja Foodi recipes from breakfast to desserts. The recipes written in this book are simple and written in an easily understandable form. The recipes start with their preparation and cooking time with the step of the instruction set. All the recipes written in this cookbook come with their nutritional values which will help you to keep track of daily calorie consumption.

happy cooking

APPENDIX RECIPE INDEX

Printed in the USA
CPSIA information can be obtained
at www.ICGtesting.com
LVHW081218140124
768656LV00008B/631